WOODSTOCK

A NEW LOOK

GREG WALTER
LISA GRANT

THE WRITERS' COLLECTIVE
Independent Books for Independent Readers

AP photographs courtesy of AP IMAGES.

Janis Joplin photo courtesy of Henry Diltz
Art Crew photo courtesy of Henry Diltz

Book Cover and Interior Design: Barbara Hodge & Lisa Grant

ISBN-13: 978-1-59411-134-1
ISBN-10: 1-59411-134-0

LCCN: 2008932371

Printed in China
10 9 8 7 6 5 4 3 2 1

Published by The Writers' Collective™ ♦ Cranston, Rhode Island

PREFACE

In 1969 I was eighteen. As you read on you'll see I was also lucky. I landed smack-dab in the middle of what was to become a touchstone of American history, culture, music and politics: Woodstock. Better to ask who *wasn't* there, than who was: Arlo Guthrie, Joan Baez, Richie Havens, Sweetwater, Ravi Shankar, Janis Joplin, Santana, Canned Heat, Grateful Dead, The Who, Sly and the Family Stone, Quill, Joe Cocker, Jefferson Airplane, Sha Na Na, and Jimi Hendrix—to name but a few. I saw them all perform on the Woodstock stage.

And I helped build that stage. I took a lot of photographs of it. Of course, being eighteen, I had better things to do than pay attention to pictures of where I'd already been. I developed the Kodachrome® slides and dumped them into a shoebox under my parents' bed.

Two years later, like many young men at the time, I fled the country rather than fight in a war I thought was wrong. Dead wrong. Some things never change.

In 1999, I was a lot older and a little wiser. I moved to California to try to recapture some of the time I had lost with my parents by leaving the country. I hadn't looked at the Woodstock photos for years and, fearing the worst, I opened the shoebox. To my delight the slides were still in good shape, though forty years did take a small toll on their brightness and contrast levels. And there was a scratch or two on some. But once I saw them I knew I had to share them with the world, along with my personal Woodstock story. My parents, my friend Alta Dena, and many others helped make that task a wonderful reality.

Why tell that story now? Because, in addition to the upcoming fortieth anniversary of one the most incredible weekends ever seen, "now" seems eerily like "then."

Once again America is at war. Once again our young men and women are dying in villages far away. And once again we live under a government wreathed in secrecy, that claims to make us safer even as the body count climbs. But also because, as we discovered on those long, yet far too brief three days in August 1969, peace, love and hope lie just around the corner.

BEFORE
THE
BEGINNING

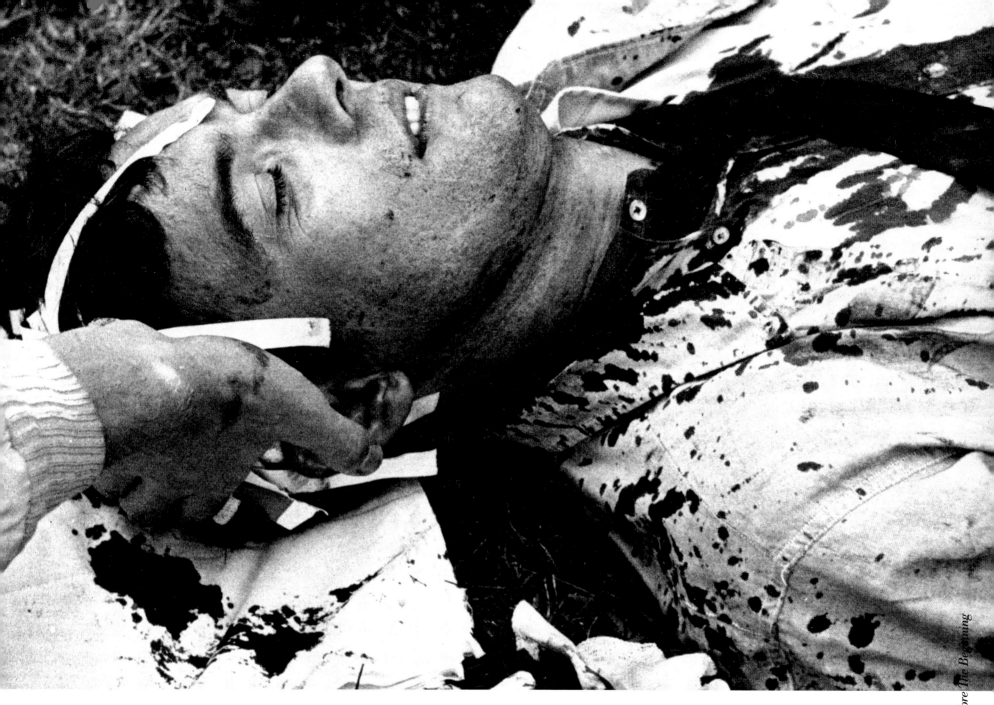

"POLICE RIOT!" SCREAMED THE HEADLINE OF THE DAILY TABLOID IN 1968.

The picture that accompanied the headline didn't have an exclamation point, but it didn't need one. A Vietnam war protester lay on the ground with blood flowing, felled by a blow from a Chicago City policeman.

The article that accompanied the photo stated that the violence stemmed from the Vietnam war protests at the Democratic National Convention in Chicago.

Chicago Mayor Richard Daley

When the growing anti-war movement became more confrontational, the establishment and the police they controlled tried to stop it with brute force—and the military.

It made no sense. The Vietnamese people were not a threat to the U.S.A. or Europe, yet to fulfill an old man's agenda thousands of our young people continued to die. But because of their so-called "drug experimentation and free-wheeling sexual exploits," it was the war's protesters who were considered immoral.

But to my peers, the true moral decay of our culture lay in its economic disparities and racial prejudices, locked in place by a military-industrial establishment that seemed hellbent on world exploitation and dominance.

The hypocrisy of America's elders paying homage to the Ten Commandments while systematically breaking every one of them was not lost on many of us.

A fellow passenger handed me a newspaper while I stood in line at Heathrow Airport, about to board the last leg of my journey from New Delhi to New York. Just seventeen-years-old, I was flying home to a country I barely recognized.

As I read the articles about the Chicago riots and stared at the horrible photos I realized I was returning to a different America than I had left.

Greg Walter in 1968

It was late August. I had been traveling around India with ten other youths as part of the World Council of Churches' Youth Encounter Program. We spent time in Mysore, Bangalore, and in the new international city of Auroville, a project started by the Sri Aurobindo Ashram and the United Nations. We also stayed a week in Calcutta with Mother Theresa and her people.

I arrived at J.F.K. Airport ten hours later. As I reentered America I saw my parents waiting for me. On the drive home they were probably concerned at how quiet I was. They had a lot of questions and wanted to hear stories about the last couple of months in their son's life, but I was too busy trying to regain my orientation to be much of a conversationalist. There was a huge cultural gap between the generations at that time, and neither side was giving much quarter.

We lived in Cornwall, a town sixty miles north of New York City on the Hudson River. It was a beautiful location, discovered centuries earlier by Henry Hudson as he sailed up the river searching for China. Located at the end of the Hudson River Valley, the town nestled against the imposing Storm King, the last mountain in the long Appalachian Chain. Cornwall had creeks, ponds, and everything else expected from a place that could have passed for a Norman Rockwell painting. The population was mostly W.A.S.P. with a few African Ameican and Jewish families, and a small group of Catholics. But it was there that I met Bobby Calvosa (p. 17), Frank Hawks (p. 58) and Rosie Cercone-Santana (p. 94).

Cornwall Memorial Day Parade, 1968

Peter Barberio playing his autoharp

The second day back from India I rose early and went off to find my friends. As I drove my mother's Opel a few people flashed me the victory sign. Only later in the day did I discover that it had become the peace sign. I hooked up with my bud Peter Barberio and we went off to party. I don't think we talked much about politics. When you're seventeen they're not exactly a priority.

"We seemed destined to become more lost than Kerouac's lost 'beat generation.'

"But through the drugs, the school, the parents, and the trying to get laid was magic. Was music.

"We held out in hick towns and the hinterlands in small enclaves of greasers, beatniks, poets and potheads, all listening to the voices of nightly FM radio.

"Then came the spring of '69, and the rumors. Then actual tickets and a quick drive on a muggy summer night in a '57 Olds.

"Suddenly it was clear to me. I was not alone. There were millions of us, a vast safety net, a nation of people with power and promise, peace, love, music, and the knowledge that we were one."

— Robert (Bobby) Calvosa, fifteen in 1969

But that fall . . .

The country elected Richard Nixon president.

My friends and I became active in the anti-war movement, mostly through the youth group of the Unitarian Church. We also sought to join organizations involved in civil rights, but that was a little more difficult due to the black communities' justifiable distrust for white people, especially a bunch of middle-class kids with long hair driving their parents' cars.

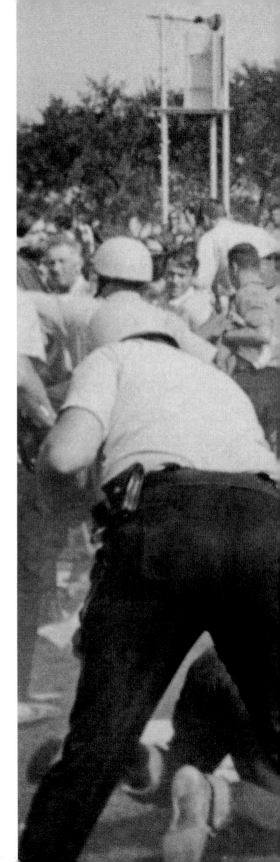

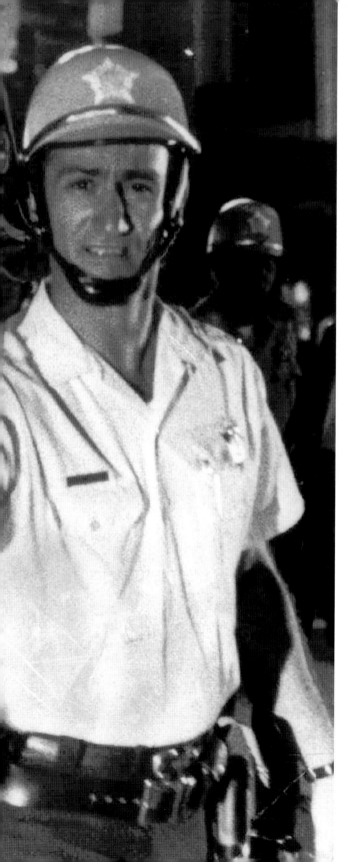

Now a high school senior, I spent most of my time finishing the academic requirements for graduation and filling out applications for colleges. But music was an important part of our sub-culture, and I played at school and anywhere else I could.

The sounds from San Francisco and England were new and exciting (subversive, according to parents), and the "underground" FM stations and alternative presses kept us informed and inspired. Day after day we read about the war and the deceptions.

A Senate Hearing would soon be convened to review the violence at the Democratic Convention.

AMAZING. THERE WAS ACTUALLY A TIME WHEN A TOY GUN COULD BE BROUGHT INTO THE SENATE CHAMBER TO MAKE A POINT WITHOUT THE BEARER BEING WRESTLED TO THE GROUND AND ARRESTED AS AN "ENEMY COMBATANT."

There were stories about new power brokers with names like Erlichman and Haldeman, updates about J. Edgar Hoover accusing all citizens with anti-war sentiments of being Communist sympathizers and traitors. The *New York Times* quoted Nixon as saying that despite protests he intended to continue his own agenda unabated. My male friends and I wouldn't have cared much about it all, except for the fact that we were the ones who would be forced to fulfill that agenda in Southeast Asia.

When I turned eighteen in February 1969, the principal summoned me to his office. As the winter sun streamed through the blinds he asked me why I hadn't registered for the draft. When I didn't answer he asked if I was scared, or was a Communist. Or did I object because of my religion? To this day I'm still not sure why I couldn't answer—or why I signed the papers he had already prepared for me. Especially since failing to register was not a crime at that time. Only refusing to report for duty if called would land you in jail.

WOODSTOCK MUSIC and ART FAIR

SATURDAY

AUGUST 16, 1969

10:00 A. M.

$7.00   Good For One Admission Only

C 02179

NO REFUNDS   GLOBE TICKET COMPANY

In the early spring I saw the first ad for an event planned for summer, one that would showcase every band whose album we'd ever heard about, or wanted to see. Every single band in one place, along with peace and art. "Mail in your money, and get your tickets in advance," the ad said. Sounded good to me.

Within a few months whenever anyone talked about what they planned to do that summer they'd say, "meet you at Woodstock," or "see you at Woodstock." "Are you going to Woodstock?" wasn't even a real question. Of course we were going. We just didn't know where it was going to be. The organizers had lost their first choice, a site near Woodstock, New York, so they moved the venue to Wallkill, a couple of hills away. Unfortunately the citizens of Wallkill didn't think that was such a great an idea.

WOODSTOCK MUSIC and ART FAIR

SUNDAY

AUGUST 17, 1969

10:00 A. M.

$7.00 Good For One Admission Only

C 01942

NO REFUNDS GLOBE TICKET COMPANY

After high school graduation Peter and I did a variety of short-term jobs, from dishwashing at a summer theatre to artificial Christmas tree manufacturing in an industrial complex. Finally Peter suggested that we go to Wallkill to get a job with the Woodstock people, who had formed a company named Woodstock Ventures. My typical response to Peter's ideas was to say "we can't do that"—which we ended up doing anyway—and to my surprise it usually worked out. So we skipped out of the factory after three whole days of working for $1.48 an hour and went to the Wallkill office, only to discover they weren't hiring.

But we hung out and tried to make sense of how they would hold a rock festival on a site that didn't have a great viewing area, didn't have a large camping area, and which was surrounded by a couple of apartment buildings and four-lane highways.

The local citizens were against the whole idea, and the lady in the office seemed stressed out. She called a temp agency to try and hire some workers to help clear the site, but apparently they didn't have anyone available. So after she hung up the phone she turned to us and said, "If you two want a job to help clear the site—for three days only—you're hired."

We showed up the next day and spent it trying to clear a path through the woods with the eleven other guys on the art crew. We built a playground out of some oak trees, spent days pushing other trees into a shredder, and eventually created a path that wasn't half-bad. Right after that we were handed our pay and told, "We don't need you anymore. Thanks, guys."

The next day Peter and I read in the paper that Woodstock Ventures had been thrown off the Wallkill site, and instead had rented the use of a farm in Bethel, owned by Max Yasgur. The farm was up north in dairy country, in the Catskills. Called the "Borscht Belt" by the New Yorkers who vacationed in its big old rambling hotels, it was a pretty area with small lakes and rolling pastures in Sullivan county near Monticello.

I wanted to keep working for Woodstock Ventures, so I talked a friend of mine, John Kopec, into applying with me. He was an art major and I figured my only chance to get hired full time was to show up with someone the art crew would like immediately.

As John and I stood at the operations trailer, off-site at the time, the same woman who'd hired me in Wallkill came out. "Hey," I said hopefully, "remember me? I worked for you down in Wallkill. Do you have any work for us?" When she hesitated I started hyping my buddy. "This is John Kopec," I said. "He's an art major, a sculptor, and…"

John kicked into charm mode. We started bantering just as the art crew showed up with the production director. One thing led to another and to my delight and surprise, we were hired and told to report for work the next week!

When we showed up a couple of days later we weren't sure what we were supposed to do or where we would stay. John and I rented an inexpensive hotel room in the White Lake area, but when we hooked up with the art crew we found out that Woodstock Ventures had reopened and rented an old hotel. It was a rickety old wooden building with no fire escapes, and seventeen miles from the festival site, but we could live there rent-free.

Our pay was a hundred and twenty-five dollars a week, which was a lot of money even without the free room and board. With overtime at the phony Christmas tree factory I would have been lucky if to make forty-three bucks a week after taxes.

John and I got a room on the fourth floor. When the fire inspector arrived a few days after we moved in he almost had a heart attack. He made sure the company fixed the fire extinguishers and the hoses, but I don't think the fire alarms ever worked.

The food, though, was incredible. Woodstock Ventures brought in two cooks from Montreal who offered us three great meals a day. Gourmet coffee, every flavor juice imaginable, fluffy scrambled eggs, freshly baked pastries and whatever other goody we might want to eat. Lunch, delivered to the site, always contained at least two huge sandwiches the likes of which I have never again tasted. Dinner was a buffet, after which we'd go over to the bar open just to us and pull a couple of cold ones. This was just during the building phase. The official policy during the event itself was no alcohol. It was one of the few rules we had.

Max Yasgur's farm was a perfect site for the festival. Within its borders was a natural amphitheater, areas for camping and an area for a heliport. The location was just right, too: far enough from heavy traffic to feel like a private space, yet close enough to the main roads to be easily reached.

The dozen of us on the art crew worked hard to get the farm ready, six and a half days a week with only Sunday mornings off. But the work itself was so much fun we didn't mind, and in the end we were the only crew that actually finished what we set out to accomplish. The crew building the fences got close. Not that it mattered. As we watched the fences rise we sensed there was no way they would serve the purpose for which they were intended, and that turned out to be true.

The first month was peaceful, but about three weeks before the show somebody must have woken up and thought, "Wait a minute. We don't have a stage." So the stage crew went into twenty-four hour a day mode, doing everything they could to get the stage built. The roof remained unfinished and the carousel that was supposed to revolve the bands onstage ended up only as a drum riser.

One afternoon Max came to visit us; we were only a few hundred yards from his barn. He was a sweet guy, and I felt he embodied the best of the older generation of Americans. They weren't all out to get us, although it seemed that way a lot of times. Max had a farmer's realism and practicality that made him shake his head in amusement as he watched the city slicker media guys come rolling onto his farm trying to grab a glimpse of what was going on.

He knew they had no understanding of what was going on, and would just turn around and go back to New York City saying, 'Guess there's something going on, but we don't really know what it is.' That afternoon Max invited us down to meet his wife and to take a tour of his happy-looking cows. It was one of the cleanest, finest dairy operations I'd ever seen. He'd come up and check on us once in a while. He was a good old dude. God bless Max Yasgur.

The art crew prepared the area in the woods that would be used by craftspeople to sell their goods. They also built the Playground, which contained some interesting structures. A totem pole made from logs and lashed together with natural hemp rope stood in the middle of the area. Three rope strands hung from the center of the six-pronged structure, and held a big flat boulder four feet off the ground. Another boulder lay on a pedestal under the suspended swinging rock. Hand-laid fieldstones surrounded the inside of the tipi structure.

What did it mean? Why was it there? Who knows. It didn't really matter. Reality wasn't the theme—life as art was. The Playground was therefore art. Why? Because we built it.

We all changed as we went through the process of creating Woodstock. It was my first real job. I'd done sports photography and freelanced this and that, but there I was, every two weeks getting a paycheck from Woodstock Ventures. We didn't have time to cash our checks, so I was able to save some money. I remember sitting on the hill in the Playground area wondering how many people were going to show up.

The Vietnam war was still raging, and we were all under a cloud of uncertainty. Assuming the event was really going to happen, we figured the site would probably max out around four hundred to five hundred thousand people.

As far as getting to the site and staying there, that was another matter.

On the Wednesday before the show I had no idea what I was going to do during the festival, and Woodstock Ventures didn't know what they were going to do with me or any of the art crew. Negotiations were on-going behind the scenes between authorities and Woodstock Ventures and who knows who and what. All the art crew knew was that we had to get our area wrapped up the next day.

On Thursday we were up at six a.m. Traffic was already starting to build on the road going to Bethel. The sun shone as I hopped into the Woodstock Ventures station wagon and cruised to the festival site to help the art crew to finish up. Thousands of people were already there. They'd been showing up for days, camping out, hanging out and checking it out.

We knocked off Thursday afternoon so we could wander around and check out the scene. I went to see The Hog Farm, a great bunch of people who had come all the way from Taos, New Mexico. They were a classic group of people, hard core. The commune, the people.

I also hooked up with my buddy Peter, his girlfriend Vickie, and a couple of other friends. I took them to the Playground, which was still a secured area.

We stood on the flat rock that hung off the tripod and swung gently back and forth looking at the three ropes intersecting with the six lines of the poles lined up against the stars as they rocked back and forth. We soaked up the magic energy of the moment before the event we all knew was coming.

By late evening I decided I'd better grab a ride back to the hotel to get some rest and maybe a bowl of soup. There were only about six people sitting in the dining room, and probably another dozen sleeping upstairs when we got back. I grabbed a bowl of soup just as somebody ran into the dining room yelling FIRE! I thought maybe it was somebody's ashtray smoldering in the lobby, but I ran to the back of the hotel anyway, where I saw three feet of flames roaring out of the basement window. The place was a Borscht Belt tinderbox, and would have gone up in flames in five minutes.

Someone grabbed one of the hoses, which fortunately worked. Because the traffic was gridlocked from the front of the hotel to Monticello, the Fire Department had to drive the fire trucks out from town on the other side of the highway. By the time they arrived we had the fire down to a dull roar and were grabbing mementos and acting like a bunch of chickens with their heads cut off. If I had been asleep on the fourth floor when fire started I probably would have died and missed the festival.

Thursday night the Motherfuckers from Manhattan hosted a free concert on the hill.

"When I arrived Thursday morning the fields were a lush green, but by Friday the long grass lay beaten into the ground. The Great Mud had began. As the stage crew worked through the night I partied with Ken Kesey, Alan Ginsberg, and Wavy Gravy. The event seems like a series of dreams.

"The days were clear. The nights were fires, lights and people. There were fools and idiots but they did not win. From the time Richie Havens began the festival with 'Concord World' the power of the music transcended everything. The spirit touched even those who were there to cause problems.

"On Sunday afternoon, after the big rainstorm and before the PA was back on, I stood in front of the stage and started singing "Let the Sunshine In." A quarter of a million people joined in. My fifteen minutes of fame.

"As the rain poured down we covered ourselves and each other with blankets, sleeping bags and whatever we could find. The hill was a river of people, water and the ever-present mud. Over the weekend I dried out my mud-caked feet in front of trash fires. And each time the clay would bake into another layer.

"The scene on Sunday was surreal, straight out of Fellini. Naked Hells Angels slid down a muddy hill, while a guy just beyond them used his wooden leg as a bong. But for most of us Woodstock was a spiritual culmination of a movement, which was to bring people together. What ignited the cause that brought us all there was beyond political. It was a time and a place that had the power to change the world.

"When Monday morning came I walked away in my clay-baked boots, bewildered. As I wandered through enormous piles of debris I wondered about what had happened and what sort of world I was going back to. When I woke up at home a few days later the entire experience seemed like a dream."

— Frank (Mazzocca) Hawks

Before The Beginning

THE BEGINNING

The Beginning

In early August Woodstock Ventures began to contract out services for everything but security. For that they brought in the professionals: members of the New York City Police Department.

If an applicant answered a question like: "What would you do if a long-hair came up and blew marijuana smoke in your face?" with a phrase like: "I'd smile and say, 'Hey, man, be careful where you're pointing that thing,'" they were hired. Nearly four hundred of them became our red-shirt security system.

But when we got to the festival site Friday morning we discovered that the officers we'd hired were in trouble. According to the Police Commissioner's rule book, they weren't allowed do outside security work. If the officers we hired showed up to work for our "hippy-dippy rock festival" up in Sullivan County, they would have to kiss their NYPD jobs goodbye.

Not surprisingly, all but four or five of them quit, which put a lot of stress on Woodstock Ventures. They in turn pressed the art crew into service, and suddenly *we* became the front line security.

A quick check of the Playground showed the fence situation to be hopeless. Since there was no time to fix it, all we could do was wonder if the event was really going to happen. That, and essentially thinking: what-the-heck-is-going-on. But there was no time for doubt; we had a job to do. I headed down to the stage area.

Our first priority was to secure the peripheral areas off the two sides of the stage. Woodstock Ventures handed out security shirts and jackets with the Woodstock logo to anyone who didn't seem too stoned and who had any kind of background in security or crowd control.

There were black shirts and jackets for the Operations Staff, red for security, and blue for the art crew and other mid-level employees. There were yellow and green shirts for concessions and sanitation. The color coding scheme turned out to be important over the next few days. It made it easy for attendees to find a Woodstock employee. And the staff could tell who was who by the jackets. Which was good, since we needed every break we could get.

The sun was shining and people were arriving in droves. We had banned alcohol sales, but people brought their own. Almost every other drug was readily available too, including bad L.S.D., unfortunately. August 15, 1969. A day that would become famous, though I didn't know it then. Someone brought me a traffic report that blew me away. Route 17, the "quick" way out of Monticello, had traffic backed up for twenty plus miles in both directions.

Forty miles of gridlock.

We had unconfirmed reports of problems on the New York State Thruway, which was over a hundred miles away.

As for traffic control, it wasn't much. New York State Police were posted at the junction of Hurd and West Shore Roads, but were not taking an active part. From what I saw and heard, their conduct during the course of the entire festival was excellent and appreciated, as was the job done by other local police, fire and emergency agencies.

In fact, it took the help of the National Guard, the U.S. Army, church organizations, and thousands of local citizens to keep half a million kids alive and safe until the festival's end. Meanwhile, the intersection of Hurd and West Shore Roads was packed with people, cars, trucks and emergency vehicles.

… and landing one hundred yards away on our improvised heliport, just up the hill from the performers' pavilion. The tent next to the heliport was to have been Woodstock Ventures staff and support's mess tent and sleeping area, but emergency evacuation services needed it more. For the rest of the weekend helicopters flew all essential performers, medical evacuees, VIP's and personnel on and off the site.

An hour later the stress began to show. People staked out their turf, physically and politically. Few people had tickets, even though no one had declared the festival to be a free event. That would come later.

The crowd exuded a mixture of agitation, anticipation and confusion. As the sun sank in the sky and clouds built up on the horizon, the stage construction crew worked feverishly among the newly arrived sound, light and movie crews. People began to hoot and holler, and everybody was wondering what the heck was gonna happen. Would it all be shut down? I heard rumors that Governor Nelson Rockefeller was about to declare the whole thing a disaster area and tell everyone to go home.

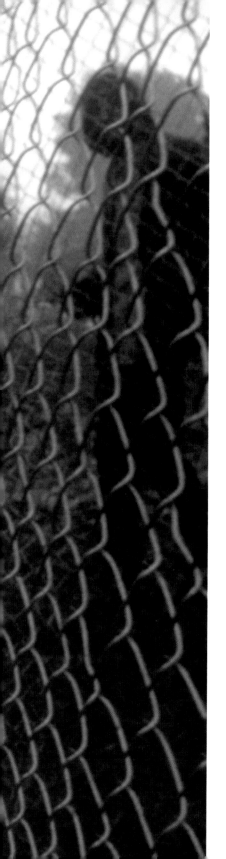

Suddenly two huge people wearing full hippie biker regalia walked through the gate and right past me. We hadn't seen many bikers. Most of us were dressed in a little bit of fringe but not many people wore beads and sandals on the East coast. The police harassed us enough as it was without our advertising our lifestyle. When those two people powered past me I knew I should say something, but as a skinny eighteen-year-old I figured there wasn't much I could do. I stayed at my post and watched the stage, where they were performing some kind of Eastern cosmic philosophy incantation. I stayed busy keeping people from entering the still open gate, and wondered if there was going to be a show.

Minutes later the two big guys came powering back up the hill, and zoomed right past me into the unsecured zone. Following them was the head of security and a few bigwig Woodstock people who wanted to know where they'd gone. "Back out into the crowd," I said, mystified. But before anyone could go after them they returned and I learned they were members of The Motherfuckers, a group from New York City who wanted to bring their group to sit in the open peripheral area. An idea security didn't like at all.

Just as the argument really got going Richie Havens started to play. I looked up. After all those months, all those radio announcements, all those "See you there's," and all the "Is it really gonna happen?"—there it was: "*High flyin' bird, flyin' way up in the sky.*"

The bikers and the security people continued to argue. "Wait a minute," I said. "Let me get this straight. You guys want to bring your people down to sit in this peripheral area?" They nodded. "But if we let everyone come down and sit in that area," I said, mad now, "why not let everybody sit here too? And if we do that, why not let everybody out there get up on stage?" That was a question they hadn't planned on answering. So the three security guys walked back down the hill, and the two biker guys went back to the unsecured area. I went back to listening to the music.

The next couple of hours were relatively normal, although we had to keep an eye on a few people who were polishing off their bottles of white, red, pink or whatever color wine they had taken to the site. Night descended quickly, though we were too busy to notice the transition. Trying to make sense of the whole thing was impossible, so everyone just did their job. Among ourselves we still had a good information pipeline about what was going on out there in the *real* world. And that was getting scary. Traffic was a total disaster. We had a lot of people coming on to the site and it was very dark.

The only secured areas were the stage, its peripheral zones and heliport, and a zone around the operations trailer at the top of the viewing area. Hog Farm camp was a self-contained island of security and comfort, and we sent the less severe cases of bad drug experiences to them. Medical personnel treated the more severe cases on site or airlifted them out. Helicopters zoomed over the crowd and landed only a short distance from the performers' pavilion. There were Woodstock Ventures helicopters, National Guard helicopters, Press helicopters and many others. The emergency vehicles, their lights flashing through the darkness, crawled through the masses on the roads at about three miles an hour.

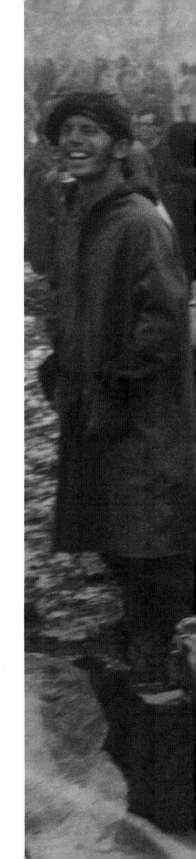

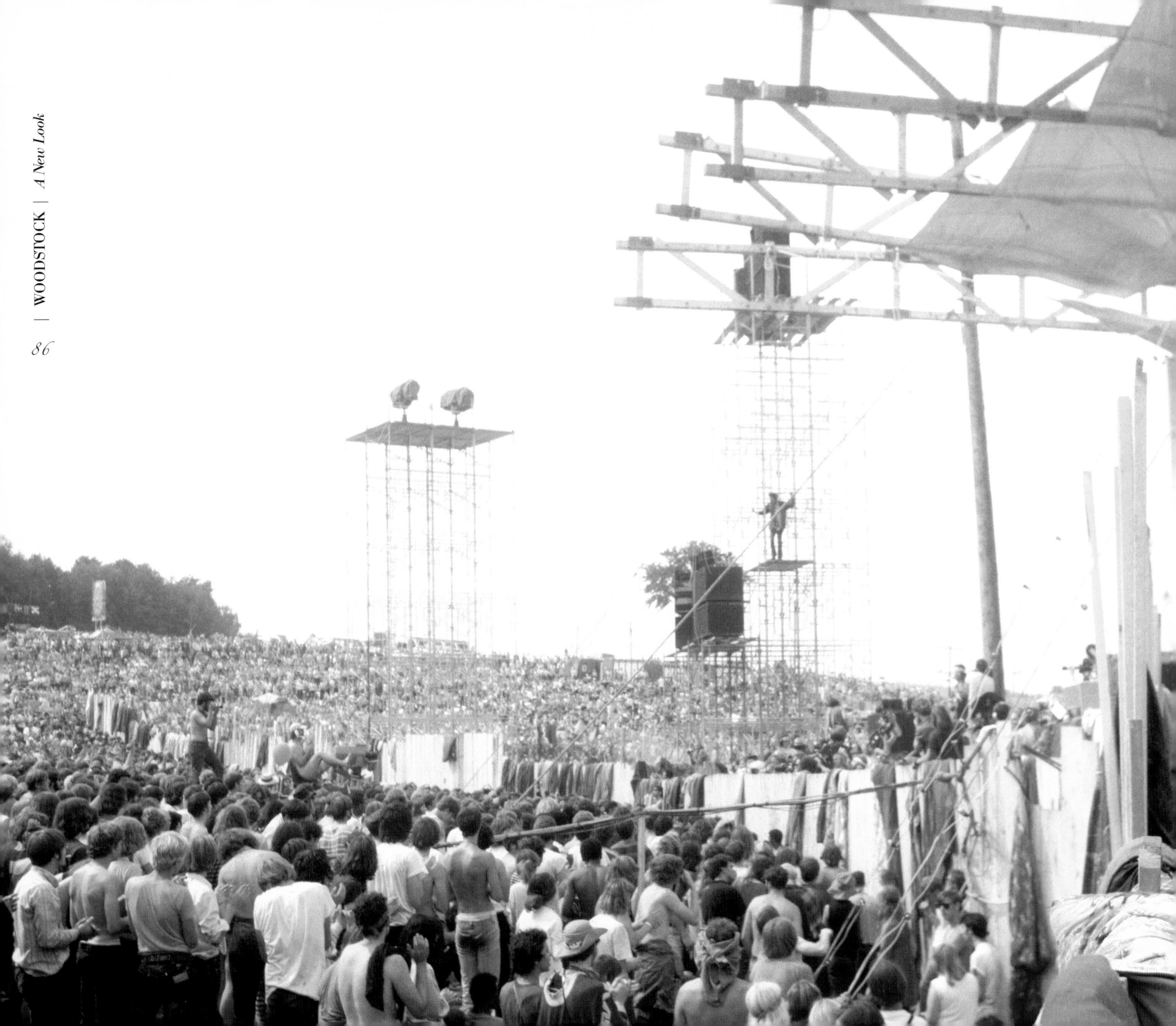

Woodstock became a free festival.

Canned Heat

That eliminated a host of problems, including political conflicts with some of our activist brothers and sisters. Shortly afterward it started to rain. Not hard, but bands that used electric instruments could not perform since there was virtually no cover over the stage. The original schedule—such as it was—called for acoustic and folk for Friday night, with rock on Saturday and Sunday.

Around eleven Joan Baez took the stage
and sang as brilliantly as ever.

During her set John Kopek and I headed over to the concession area to check things
out. Security told us to keep moving and find things we could fix, while ignoring
what we couldn't. Our motto was supposed to be: If you can't fix it, forget it. That
meant that to a large extent people would just have to take care of themselves and
each other.

Just then someone spotted our Woodstock jackets and ran over. "Where's the emergency hospital?" he said. "We've got a guy that took some bad acid." Four people walked by carrying a guy who was rigid as a board. His eyeballs rolled back into his head as the strychnine contracted every muscle in his body, and the psychedelic opened his mind so there was no avoiding the pain.

We pointed in the direction of the crew tent, and they went away into the darkness. After checking the concession area we headed over to the crew tent ourselves, where there was hot food and coffee twenty-four hours a day. As we sipped our coffee we could hear the screams of people in the emergency evacuation area who had taken acid at the wrong time of their lives. The people that arrived that night didn't really know where they were, but despite rain, scary helicopters, hordes of people and traffic backed up forever—we all survived the night.

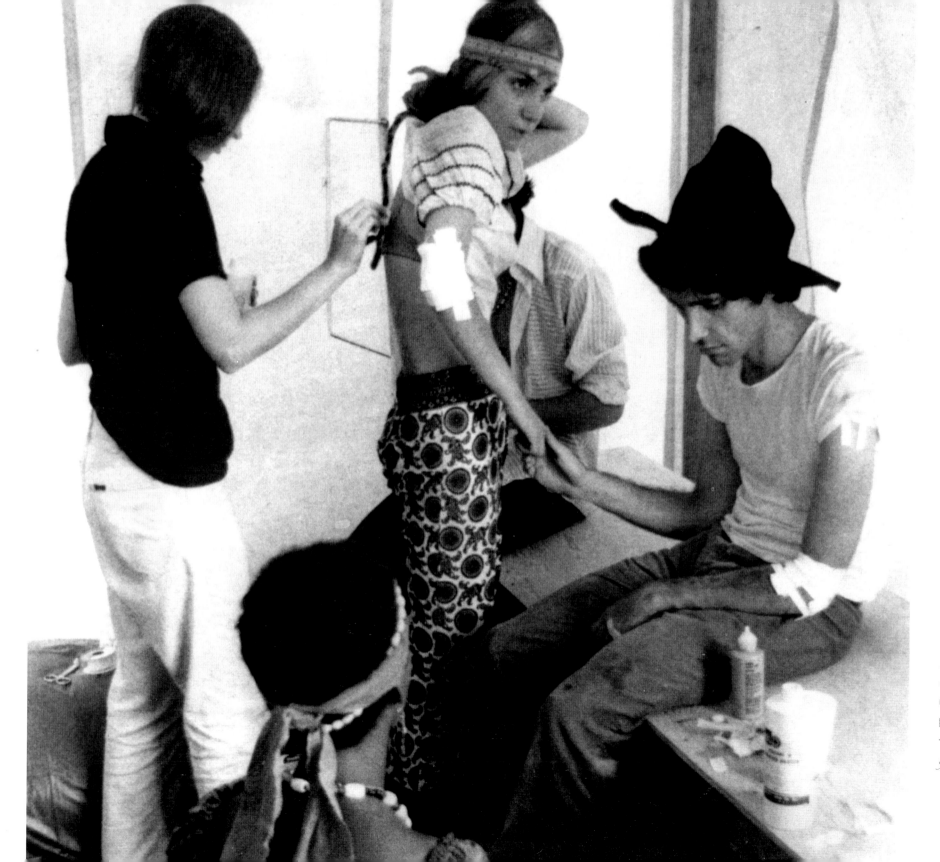

"The Woodstock tickets were a sweet sixteen birthday gift from my brother, who was two years older.

"How he talked my Mom and Dad into saying it was okay still strikes me funny. Had they known the festival would attract 500,000 people, I would have never of been permitted to go, and would have had to watch the pandemonium unfold on the nightly news with the rest of the country.

"As I walked towards the concert ground with the huge crowds, time ceased to exist. People were beautiful to one another, friendly, giving, and helpful. It got late and someone offered their tent for me and my friend Terry to crash in. I remember watching in awe the unbelievable performances of Santana, The Who, Richie Havens (who sang endlessly), The Dead, Jefferson Airplane, and so many more.

"The announcements were continuous: who lost who, who was waiting at the Red Cross station, who got married and who overdosed. Your business was everybody's business. When John Sebastian played, a camera zoomed in on Terry and me and captured us listening to him play. We found out later it was a moment featured in the Woodstock Festival movie—our only claim to fame!

"We stayed till the end; wet or muddy, we didn't care. I wanted to see the legendary Jimi Hendrix play The Star Spangled Banner. It was definitely a case of best saved for last; the most spectacular sight and sound I have ever seen or heard. When I listen to the classic music of that time, and envision the most memorable moments of the concert, I get chills down my spine. And I close my eyes and say, I was there. Really there."

— Rosie Cercone-Santana

Rosie

Joe Cocker

Luckily, the two Woodstock Ventures owners had their affairs in order. Michael Lang was not about to deny history, so John Roberts kept writing checks. And there were a lot of checks. It didn't take the bands long to realize that when they signed the contracts it wasn't just to play at the festival but to let those performances be recorded and filmed. Turned out to be just as big a deal as a million dollar movie budget.

Saturday was a lot of fun, especially since the weather cooperated. Keef Hartley came on early and rocked. Late in the afternoon an unknown West Coast band took the stage: Santana. Within minutes they lifted the crowd to another level. No one on the East Coast had ever heard a beat like that. A lot more people showed up for the 11 p.m. show.

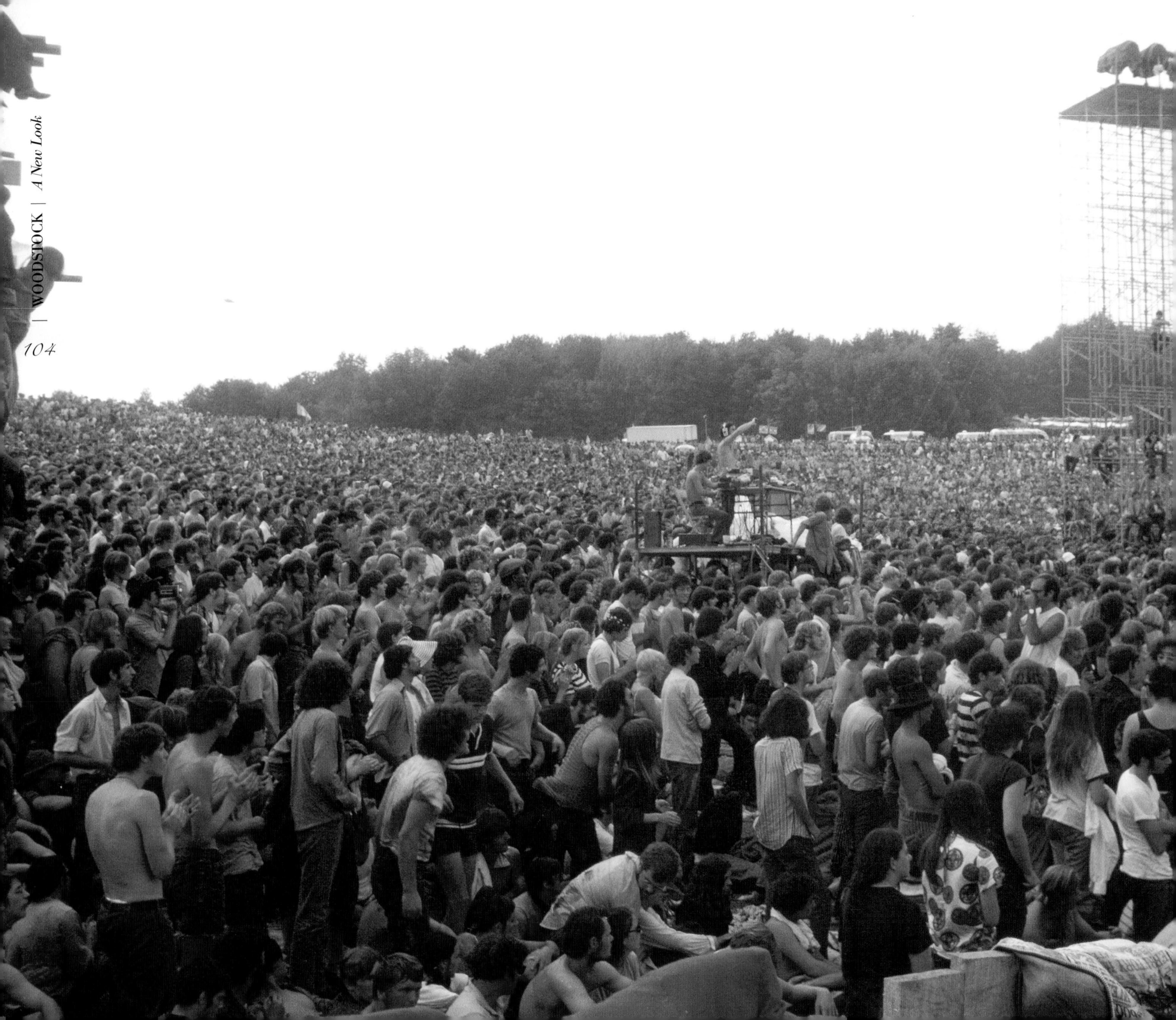

During the Grateful Dead set, John Kopek and I stood next to the fence that enclosed the peripheral stage areas. "Outside that wooden fence are four hundred thousand people," he said. "They're packed like sardines and pushing it. It might fall over." Much as I'd been enjoying myself, this put me in a whole other frame of mind. The day had been fun, but the idea of nearly half a million people in one small place was scary.

While the Grateful Dead were on John and I decided to explore. As we walked up the road just beyond the compound, helicopters flew over our heads. It was dark and crazy and there were masses of humanity on the move. By the time we got back the Dead had finished their set, there was no music or announcements coming from the stage, and a lot of people—about a hundred thousand—left the viewing area. That loosened things up. Everyone else stayed for the duration of the show, and what a show it turned out to be.

At nearly one o'clock in the morning, and after a good forty-five minutes of silence from the stage, a single note rang out from the lead guitar of the Creedence Clearwater Revival. The stage lights seemed to turn to crystals. I could see every pixel of energy that rose from the two spotlights shining on John Fogarty, and every atom from each of the three hundred thousand people on the field behind us felt in sync. Every musician. Every person on stage. Every human with eyes to see and ears to hear The Note. Then Creedence Clearwater Revival played. They played understandable, danceable, clean, clear American music.

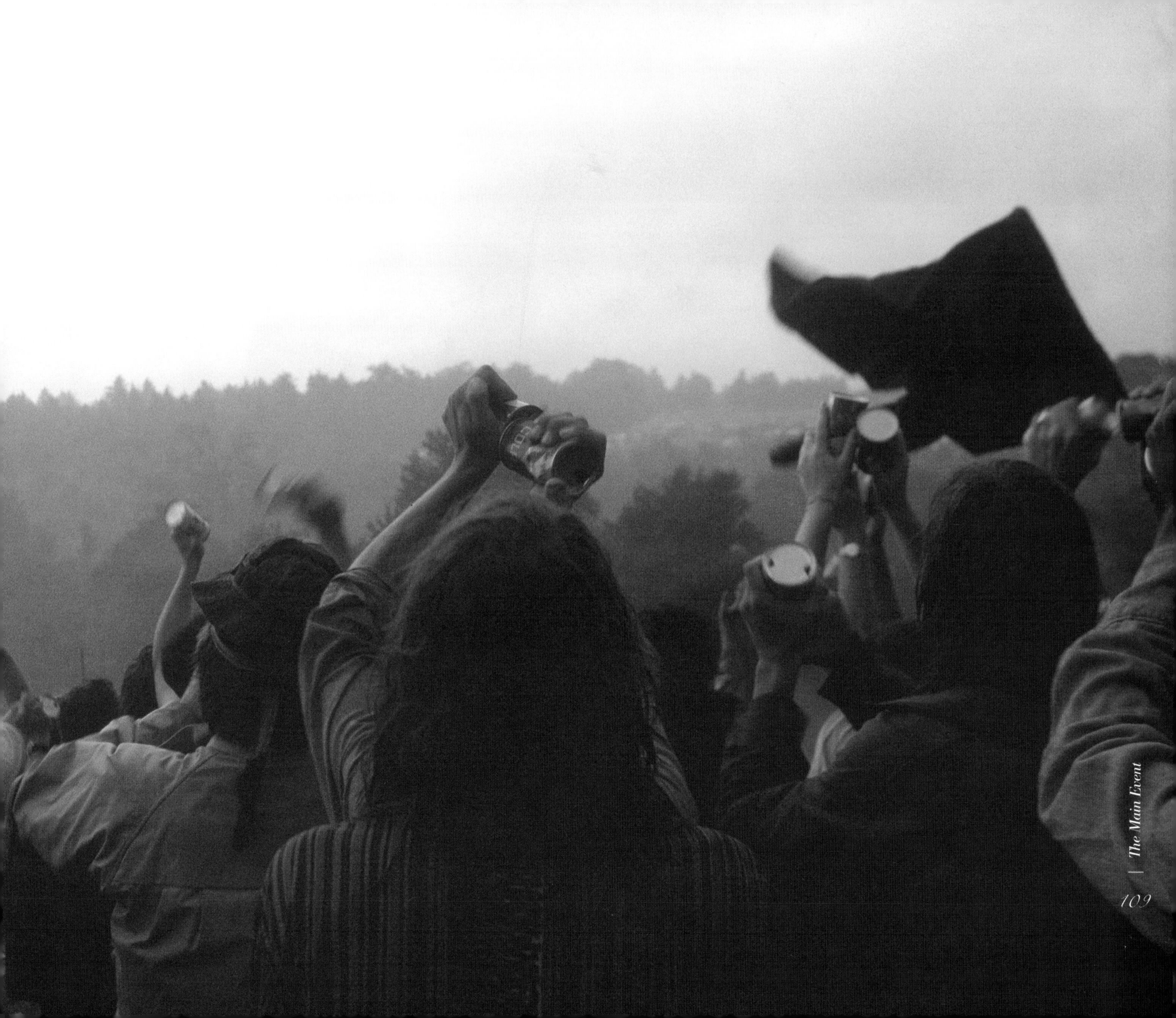

... WHO KNOWS WHAT ELSE WENT ON IN THE CROWD?

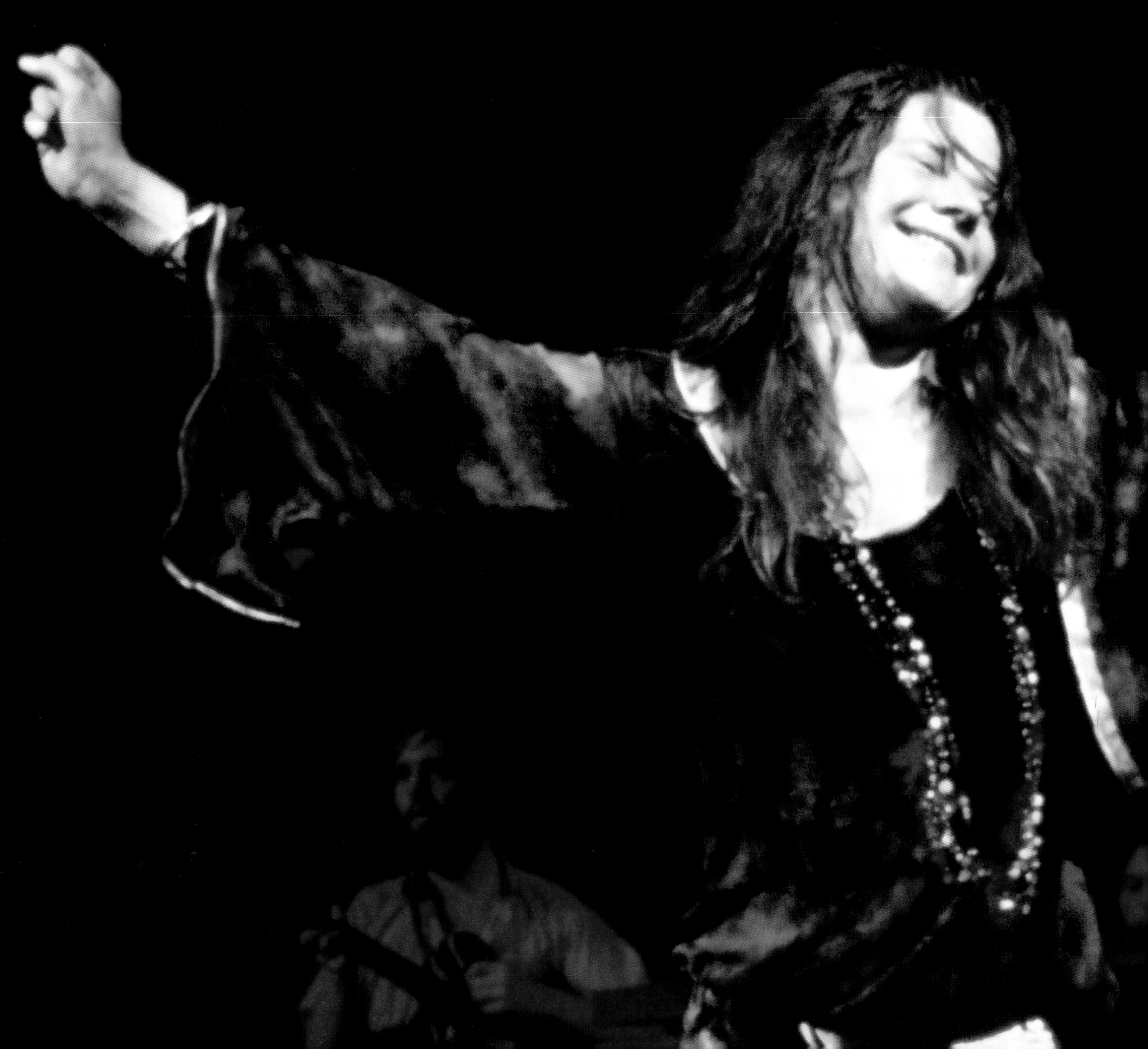

And then there was the incomparable Janice Joplin, who came to share her soul.

The music captured my soul from that one magic note onward, to every light flash and psychedelic projection screen reality. Helicopters continued to fly overhead. Masses of humans were on the move. The Who came on and drove us all to ecstasy. People screamed and danced and lit matches, and grooved far into the cold, dark early morning hours.

I headed to the photographers' pit to make sure nobody climbed up over the fence or onto the stage. I was a few feet away from Roger Daltrey when I noticed a guy next to me with no identification. He had no Woodstock jacket, no badge, or an artist's pass. No camera, no notebook, and no tape recorder either. He did have fuzzy hair, glasses, and one of the biggest smiles I'd seen all day.

The Who came on and drove us all to ecstasy.

See me ... feel me ...

touch me ... heal me.

Pete Townshend

The Who rocked. They played most of *Tommy*, their new opera. Keith Moon was incredible. Roger Daltrey was living the part. It was the first North American performance after their recording. It was so fresh. So in context.

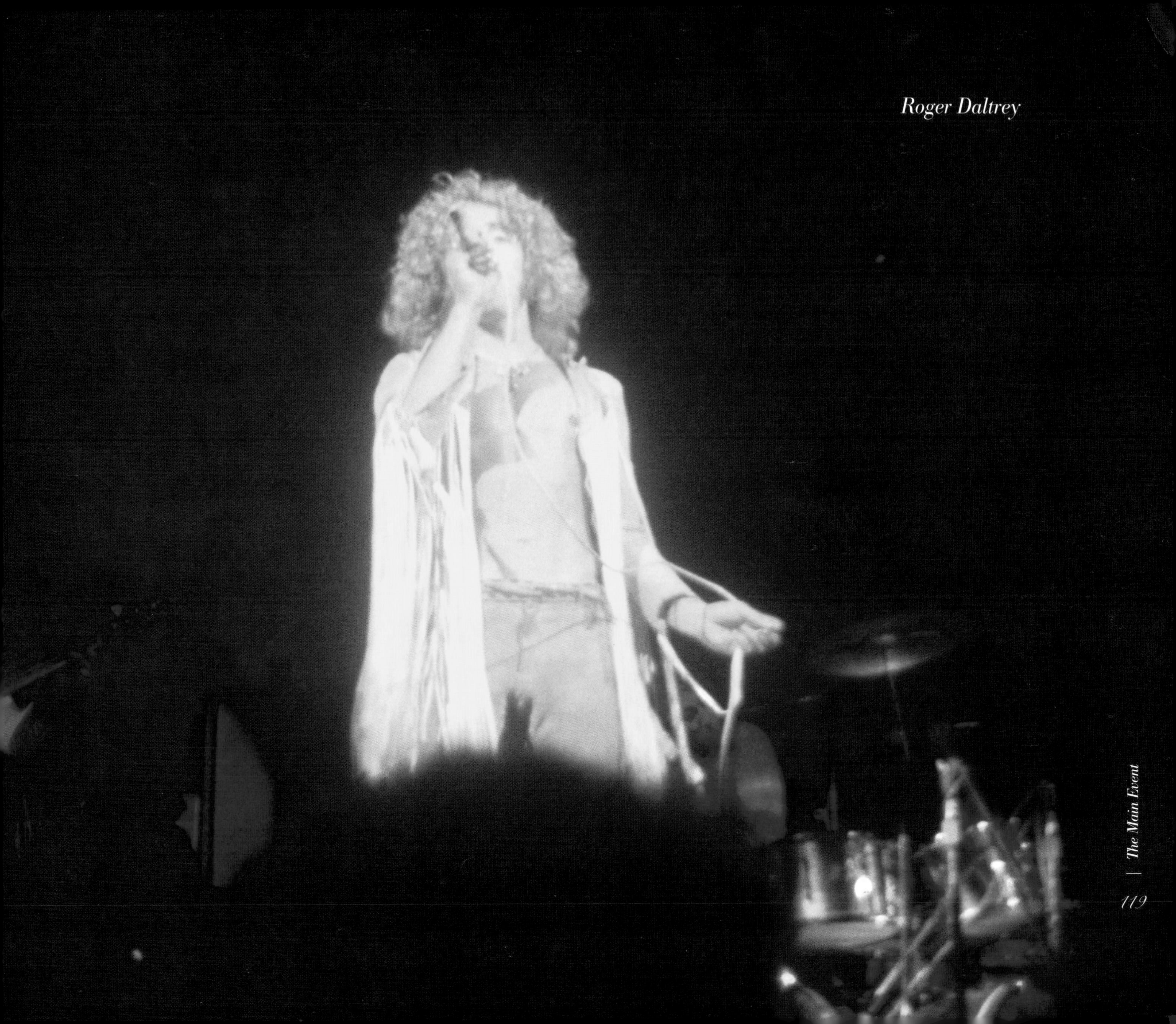
Roger Daltrey

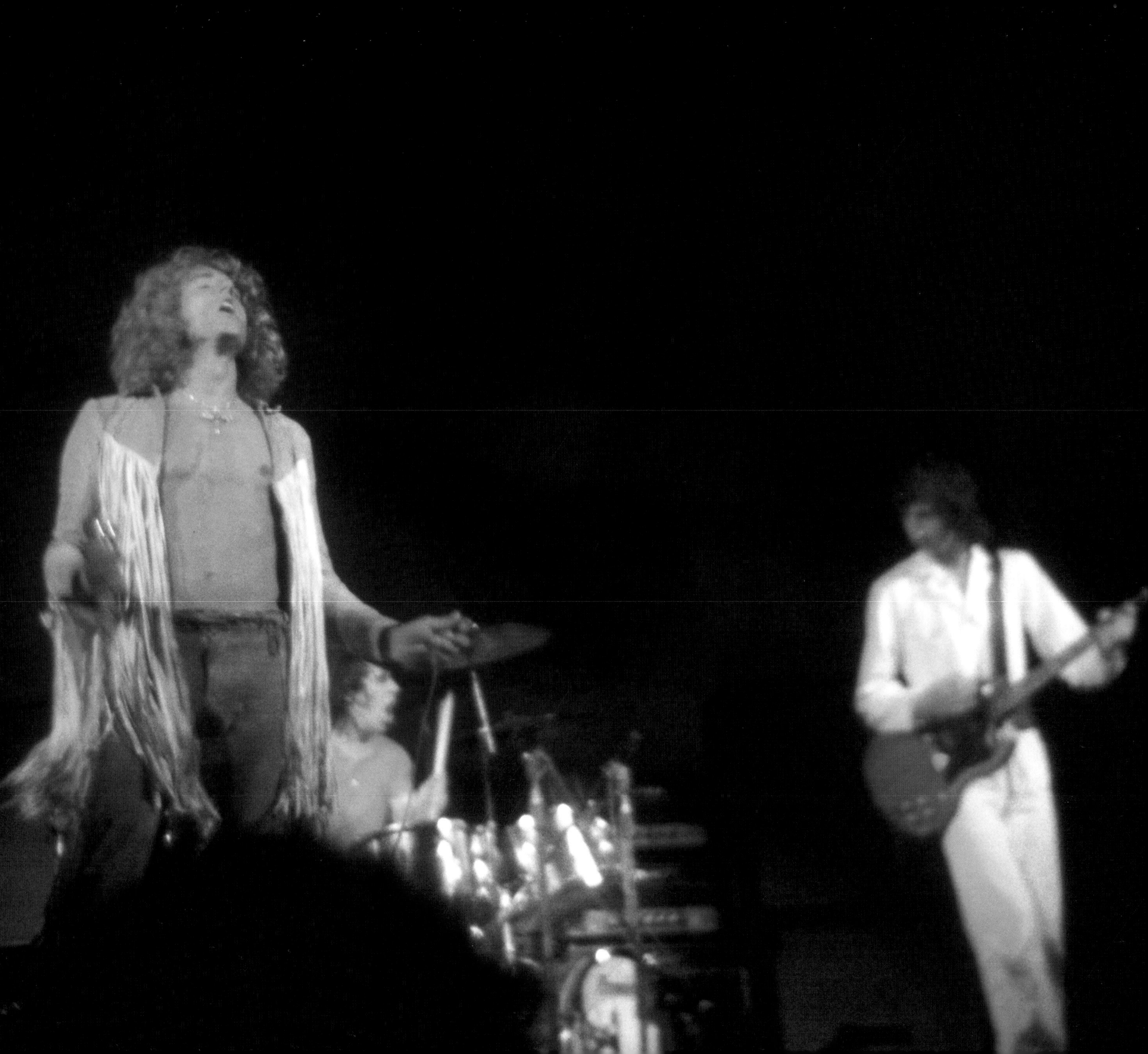

Dawn broke behind the band and people looked right and left, discovering who they had been standing next to in the darkness for the last eight hours. It created an instant bond most of us would never know again. Then it was over. The Who wrapped their set, said, "Thank you very much," and headed off to party.

SUNDAY

WE'LL NEVER
BE THE SAME

Sunday: We'll Never Be the Same

Grace Slick and Jefferson Airplane

Grace Slick, fresh from the great city of San Francisco, home of the Summer of Love, took the stage. "Are you ready for some morning maniac music?" she asked. The crowd roared, "Sure!" So on we rocked.

As Jefferson Airplane finished their set I strolled up the hill and into the woods. I walked past craft sellers and gypsies as the rising sun slanted through the poplars. There was peace in the woods that morning.

Some time later I headed to the main viewing area. A young man in his twenties came over. "I think I just killed someone," he said. His face was pale, and his eyes showed terror and shock. I was too stunned to do more than send him to the operations trailer, and I heard later that he had accidentally driven his tractor over someone asleep on a farm road. It was one of only two fatalities that weekend. The other was a drug overdose. Amazing statistics for four days of half a million people camping out with few services.

In the afternoon John and I drove the staff Chevy to the operations trailers. Clouds rolled in over the hills and it got dark. Mean-looking dark. Then it rained. And hailed. The windows steamed up as we watched tens of thousands of people slip and slide in the mud, trying to find cover. Bodies and faces crawled past the car, but we couldn't let them in. It was like being in a bomb shelter during a war.

We were all over the festival site the rest of the day, but by ten-thirty that night it was really cold and I didn't feel the magic anymore. The lights were still on, but somehow they weren't the same.

By then most of the "beautiful people" had left, but there were still people hanging out. I was tempted to stay and see Jimi Hendricks, but there was no way I'd make it till morning. I went back to the hotel and slept right through to Tuesday.

Story... We'll Never Be the Same

When I woke I went back to the site. There wasn't much left except a mountain of garbage. I stayed on with the few staff people who remained, and helped to clean up for another couple of weeks. We fixed fences and hung out on Yasgur's farm, where bulldozers piled up the trash into heaps for burning. Eventually the grass sprang back up out of the mud.

Friends asked me to stay with the tour and go to the upcoming Texas Pop Festival. Afterward they'd continue across Canada by train. That road would have taken me to Altamont, the alpha and omega of the rock festival movement. I declined the offer and opted for college instead. I said goodbye to Woodstock and picked up my final check. It beat the wages at the Christmas Tree factory.

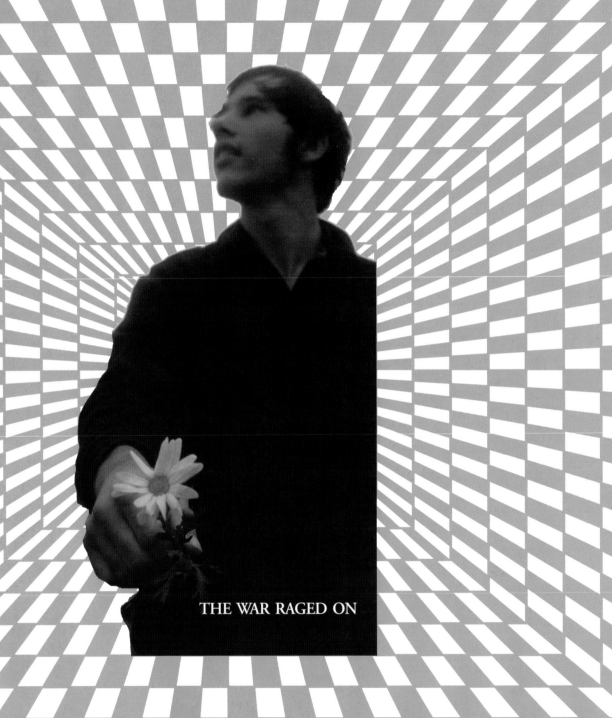

THE WAR RAGED ON

AFTERWORD

I finished working for Woodstock Ventures in late August. Unfortunately, my draft status was 1A, and in 1971 I pulled a low number in the Selective Service System lottery, which meant a call sooner rather than later. When I was younger I'd wanted to attend the U.S. Naval Academy and serve in the Air Corps, but I couldn't justify going to Vietnam. I didn't believe a military victory was possible and couldn't even remember the rationalization for being there in the first place. I supported our troops but believed that the war was a waste of our generation and our country's resources. I couldn't claim conscientious objector status though, because I would not swear that I would never fight in any war. Some wars, like WWII, were worth fighting.

By the time 1971 was half over, I had met and married my wife, Renee, in California, and we'd moved with friends to upstate New York. A week later I received my induction notice. I was to report to the Induction Center, where following a pre-determined physical I was to become a member of the United States Army or Marine Corps. Did I pay attention to reality? Obey the order? Nope. I ignored the situation and continued to travel, play music and enjoy life. A bunch of us flew to Amsterdam in early November, broke but happy.

Two days later I learned that a Federal Grand Jury had indicted me for Draft Evasion, a felony punishable by five years in prison and a ten thousand dollar fine. The knowledge that I was now a political refugee without legal status anywhere in the world was frightening. But I had friends, and the counter-culture gave me strength. By mid-May Renee and I arrived in Calais, France. We were out of money and Renee was pregnant. My parents generously sent us a money order and offered to get us to Canada, and we felt that with a child on the way that would be the safest course. We were welcomed as landed immigrants, and given help to raise our two children. Thank you, Canada—a great and gracious country.

In 1977 Jimmy Carter granted me and sixteen hundred others still under indictment a full and unconditional pardon.

During the next few years I visited friends and family, made music, and became reacquainted with my country. And my memories. Woodstock has become a legend, a potent symbol of empowerment the likes of which we will probably never see again. The nearly half a million souls who battled traffic, rain, mud and other hardships to come together, to be transformed by the music, the place and one another, discovered how strong they could be. I hope that people who were there will recall their own memories when they read this book, and regain the power they had. Or if they were not there, that they will draw upon Woodstock's magic and imagine what still can be.

Greg Walter, Woodstock
October, 2008

IS THIS YOURS?

The hunt to find the $5000 Great American Tush is on! Prove "The End" is yours, and claim your $5000. Just fill in the form and send it with your proof (stories and/or photos), postmarked by June 30, 2009 to:

Woodstock Great American Tush Award
780 Reservoir Ave., STE 243
Cranston, RI 02910

No phone calls or faxes will be accepted. No entries will be accepted online*, but once you've sent in your form and have received an email confirmation, you can then send a YouTube video proof link to us for uploading. Site members will be allowed to vote for the 10 Finalists, who will be "revealed" on July 15, 2009. However, the Publisher's decision as to whether or not we have found "The End" will be final. "The End" will be announced on August 15, 2009—Woodstock's 40th Anniversary—and the $5000 will be awarded then.

*Incomplete entries will be discarded.

For details, go to: www.TheWoodstockBook.com/GAT

Name: _____ Phone: _____ Email: _____

Street Address: _____ City: _____ State: ____ Zip: _____

Type of proof enclosed: _____ Will provide YouTube Video ❑ Yes ❑ No

By signing and submitting this form, Entrant agrees that: Proof submisions will not be returned; and that all the information contained on the form and in the submitted Proof is true; and that the Entrant is the sole owner of the rights to this Proof, which has not been assigned, pledged or otherwise encumbered; and that the Proof is original, has never before been published as a whole or in part in any form, is not in the public domain in any country, and does not infringe any copyright or any other proprietary or personal right; and that the Proof contains no material that is libelous, in violation of any right of privacy or publicity, or harmful so as to subject The Writers' Collective (hereinafter known as the "Publisher") to liability to any third party or otherwise contrary to law. The Entrant further agrees to grant to the Publisher, without reservation, exclusive worldwide rights to the Proof, and acknowledges that the Publisher may use the Proof as is or changed as needed, in all Media for all time, in all Languages and for all Promotion worldwide without exception. In the case of being awarded the $5000, Entrant agrees to be responsible for all Federal, State and Local taxes, and Entrant agrees to make themselves available, without further compensation, to any national, state or local media, and for all promotional purposes.

Signature: _____ Date: _____